GOODBYE LYRIC

poems

GOODBYE LYRIC

The Gigans & Lovely Gun

Ruth Ellen Kocher

The Sheep Meadow Press

Rhinebeck, NY

All inquiries and permission requests should be addressed to the publisher:

The Sheep Meadow Press
PO Box 84
Rhinebeck, NY 12572

Cover art courtesy of Krista Franklin:
"The Two Thousand & Thirteen Narrative(s) of Naima Brown" (Installation)
Author photograph: Patricia Colleen Murphy
Designed and typeset by The Sheep Meadow Press
Distributed by The University Press of New England

Library of Congress Cataloging-in-Publication Data

Kocher, Ruth Ellen, 1965-
  [Poems. Selections]
  Goodbye Lyric : The Gigans & Lovely Gun / Ruth Ellen Kocher.
     pages cm
  Includes bibliographical references.
  ISBN 978-1-937679-31-6
  I. Title.

PS3561.O313A6 2014
811'.54--dc23

                        2013034486

CONTENTS

On First Looking into Ruth Ellen Kocher's Gigans

Form is both a revolution and an evolution. It's a furtive hand, striking into the darkness, taking something animal, something mineral, those stealthy materials activated by the breath and the blood, and giving them shape, meaning and, yes, immortality. Form is an activation of the mind, a blissful burden; a shaping designed to omit and to amplify, to engage and to satisfy.

Admit it: we like form—as postmodern and forward thinking as we claim to be in post-20th Century letters. We like the curl of a wave, the shape of a hip, the bulge of a bag full of books. There's been a resurgence in what's known as "traditional" poetic forms—anthologies and collections of sonnets, sestinas, pantoums, villanelles and all manner of repeating French forms. There are marvelous experiments that have taken hold in in the classroom (Jim Simmerman's "Twenty Little Poetry Projects") and forms invented to mock traditional forms (Billy Collins's paradelle, invented as a joke, soon proved irresistible to many, and before you could say "mockery," poets were writing "real" paradelles, with much to say). Establish writing communities found continuity in newly invented forms, such as the bop, invented by Afaa Michael Weaver for the Cave Canem Workshops, and the kwansaba, invented by Eugene B. Redmond, who for decades led community-based workshops in East St. Louis, Illinois.

Into this heritage and legacy comes Ruth Ellen Kocher's gigan. Its prosody is simple, as the poet herself explains:

The gigan prosody, if you need to know, is couplet / tercet / couplet / couplet / couplet / tercet / couplet — line 1 repeats as line 11; line 6 repeats as line 12; final couplet is a volta.

But what that simple prosody can do, in the hands of a poet as gifted as Ruth Ellen Kocher, is tremendous. This form sings with subtle music, muses on any number of subjects, and makes us slow our roll, appreciate and anticipate the lyric nature of our language in a concentrated, elegant way.

My favorites of the gigans give me that certain poetic thrill none other than Emily Dickinson spoke of: "If I feel physically as if the top of my head were taken off, I know that is poetry." As executed by Ruth Ellen Kocher, there's a lushness to the form, an unabashed sensuality that I find lacking in a lot of contemporary poetry. The gigan makes you lick your lips, happy to be a reader of poetry again.

The form allows Kocher to be dreamlike but not obscure, passionate but never obvious about those passions. For example, in "Treaty" the poet begins:

> last night my chest opened like a house
> swinging the front doors back on their hinges

The form's initial couplet invites and intrigues. I admire the gigan's "set-up"—that inviting initial couplet followed by a sturdy tercet, then a series of three couplets, and finally a concluding couplet that serves as a volta:

> do you hear the savanna's grasses   rattling the wind like a cage
> the sound of those beasts grazing   each pace of feral plain

There's a charge to the end of a gigan—a jolt of feeling, a lash of electricity. It's a form that is both expansive and terse, a space of for a little story with a lot of meaning. It may remind some readers of the Japanese haibun—a form that combines prose and haiku—in that it has the capacity for story and the compression of verse. It's a little world that contains multitudes.

With this collection, Ruth Ellen Kocher has written the most beautiful guidebook for her gigan form. As a poet, I can't wait to try the form myself. With these sure and sensitive poems, any poet can cull the needed inspiration to attempt the form. As a reader though, I'm just grateful to have the chance to peek into her ample and wondrous imagination, to dwell in the house of Ruth Ellen Kocher's devising, to hear her gigans sing and swing, to listen as this poet listens to the natural world she inhabits:

> listen to the cardinal cutting a racket through my neighbor's pine
> hear his salutation   his winged confirmation music   un-stilled

Allison Joseph
Carbondale, IL
September 2013

55 GIGANS & 5 NOTES

Candor

i would give up anjou pears for you   and their cousins
the bosque   which are more beautiful   wrapped ochre

wrapped gold around their small deaths   wrapped securely
as though they know an old friend will call   say *yes*   say
no   and this old friend   he would die for a crust of earth

peeled back to reveal some buried bliss   a dance of bees
singing out the ruined pleasure of battle   their lavish

avenues of forsythia   their swank arias of roses   inked roses
sung roses   that want most to be the silk worm's slink and cower

pity them   their faithless world   their bruised
and darkening red   i would give up anjou pears for you

i would peel away their splendorous backs   reveal the equation
we build our hunger upon   the dank musk of decay turned sweet
the soil's woe begotten centuries mulched into pollen   nectar

think of the silk worm's desire   its dreams of mulberry leaf
its singular drive toward the green silhouette of rapture

Ingather

suppose the cut roses   understand their own
lush   cliché   so their arrogance

resists   thirty panes of daylight
filtered through   dirty windows   curls
the black molder   at their beautiful luxury

to convince you   you are loved
the metro link barrels through   sunday

two weeks ago   when you pocketed each
imagined tenderness   the roses   not yet cut

their deaths   not yet certain
the vase catching no light bright enough

to convince you that you are loved
your heart read the colorful   confetti of painted tiles
on the train stop's walls   as celebration

downtown   the sky   burst in tapered explosions
as though   the fireworks were longing ignited

Rune

he believes she is the age of smoke and honey   says her name like   *sister*
lies on the couch by the window   reading her words   as though

written for him   the assembled resonance   syllabic pull   the stutter
repetition   the constructed lilt of vowels which might soften
the hard edge of each 'c'   or wax an 'r' into deference

he dreamed once between them a garden   a flume   greens and pinks
littering soil   abandoned lot   bristled sweet   the words

mean nothing to the dead dog in the road   nor the gardener
the tractor across the lawn   to the cop downtown   a vague

taste of coffee in his mouth   on the couch by the window he dozes
on her tongue   imagines an age of loam and salt moves in the circuitous

way of water pooling   dreams a single bee emerges from her throat   pulls
itself out of her dark mouth   surfaces at the edge   her bottom lip
followed by another   then another   her every thought swarms

takes his eyes for magnolia blooms   his ears roses   his cheeks
the layered fullness of camellia flowers expelling un-metered breath

Excursion

the dream goes like this   first the sky ascends into that gloom
behind blue   then the soil falls away   not all at once

piece by piece   car by car   each blade of grass refracts its own
sunny glare   then the ground's disappearance   the trees' bare
roots hang momentarily   their trunks becoming the carriage of a body

whose soul withdraws   and then   before they all give to the nothing
the world makes   i wake next to soft snoring   his open mouth

the blindness of our bodies not quite touching   i realize a savage
disappearance   the thirst of eclipse   his fork disappearing into

his mouth   his footsteps i hear in the hallway   moving further and further
away   the last wine spilled   the dream goes like this   comes like this as well

if the world exists   it succumbs to the nothing i make of this night   it opens
its mouth and yawns blue mornings into the clutter of freeways
and midwestern storms   into pomegranate crushed and staining my sink

into churches whose caramel oak doors swing wide   the laughs
of the living inhabiting them   their arias   their hymns   their sure ways

Racket

one day on the road   you will meet a lonely suspicion   it will wink at you
admire your strong legs   it will brush up against your side and even

within the wind's sheer whistle   you will hear it *purrrrr* suspicion has a beautiful
mind   all fractions and orbits   postulates and inertia   it will tell you *the speed*
of light is the same regardless of the frame of reference of the observer

and you will understand   as though a new scent unfolds itself   within your
exhaled breath   you will comprehend as if the lark's call   becomes a sudden

and explicable grammar   as if suspicion itself   guides you by the hand to
the last unoccupied table in the bar   where a chair waits   anchors itself

to task   feels your weight become its single burden   your chore
is simple   one day on the road you will meet   a charming suspicion

let it sniff the nape of your neck   understand then   as though a new taste
flutters upon your tongue   steels itself against the hunger   you have always
had for haplessness   and tragedy   for the monsoon raking its thunder across sky

for the crippled wren   that can't escape its slash   and strike   but
the road winds ahead   anyway   its sandy reach   its endless stay

(first note)

consider an elegy for the five   * * *   * *

ways

the night

                                        imagines

undoing us as we
sleep

Cull

the first red leaf has fallen from an old
maple bucking the sidewalk   the concrete

risen to its bark circling the base
in the angle of praying hands   or shifting
ice breaks on the lake   or logs rearing

one over another   their last journey
down river   it is the way our passing makes

itself known in the geometry of simple things
i imagine you in a far away city instead of here

next to me   wonder in which place i would love
you more or less   imagine each red leaf fallen

a testament to the way we rise   circle our place
of origin   rear our backs to one another so
we breathe the knot of neck and shoulder

in the depth of that tree is a sweet goodbye   a plank
a wood-block   a heartbreak waiting to be felled

Aversion

the autumn star shows up tonight off the moon's low
left quadrant   but the trees deny their season   full green

only just now . shedding lush more daily
tops thick yet   weightless   the sun finds a brown
haze   hungers at their leaves   i cannot be more full

of summer than they   so desperate for the season's
clutch to unravel dissipating hush   for the grackles

to come once more as lovers   departed   then
returned   the small yellow feet clutching each branch

within a shrieked embrace   is this the time that begins
our longing   when the autumn star shows itself needling

the night   desperate as the trees for the sun flared spell
to extinguish itself   to say   *i will leave you   i will leave you*
i will leave   as we are all left eventually without desire

the trees' arms will be empty as mine in three short
months   will cut jagged lines from the flat winter sky

Purview

you imagine you are   made of glass   the thought
does not   depart from your daily   life

your wisteria out of season   the dim   dogwood
shedding berries   your chipped   failing walkway
to a front door   that is not yours

at night   you settle into   an opaque fullness
the inside of you   belongs to you

in the morning   the light   always there
turns out your silent   recesses   strips you bare

a flirtation of refraction   and transparency
you imagine   you are made of glass

at night   again   understand the invisible
fill yourself with   blindness   and stars
open your mouth   to the silver

vowel   the moon would make   if it spoke just
once   if its reflection could   estimate sound

Fledged

in the distance a dog cries as dogs do   deeply like a woman cries
as though her heart   blood full   rakes itself perpetually against glass

and like the woman   he breeds a bottomless sorrow   a millennium
of languishing alongside our uprightness   our smoking fires   our beautiful
agile hands   our affectionately subtle compartments of we and they

but the dogs   how sad for us to have stood and left them there on all
fours   how they longed for our snouts buried in soil next to them   how

they pitied our loss of bristling fur   and when the air no longer carried
the herd of bison moving north   the sniff of storm sweeping the plain's

pollen over the western ridge   when the air lost its electric green scent   its tinge
of sweat   its quiet dimension of piss and spit   the dogs cried   as dogs do   into

our future   disheartened for us to have stood   forgotten our way
their jaws tighten toward the moon to which they offer
apologizes on our behalf   long hollow vowels wrapped around a forever

mourning   they cry so much like a woman who knows the truth folded
neatly into her life   *o-o-ooh* they cry   *o-o-ooh* they cry

Loom

i imagine my death as anyone's death
satellite image of a torn car   a hospital sheet

creased carefully around   my feet   its lovely
tucked corners   a bleached resistance to   the wet echo
my lungs fit into   the wanting room

in this moment   you will hate me
the way truth   crouches to drink from the clear

surface of my face   free   from any rippled disturbance
and beneath   algae's density increases

exponentially   i cannot help but become you
and so imagine my death as yours

in that moment you will hate the grass
you will despise the trout silvering an imagined stream
reject the stoic agency of apricots   realize a beautiful flaw

each pit a perfect loss   the ground rises   the fruit yellow
fleshed   remembering   earthworm   compost   fall

Vantage

lonely says the streets of morocco tinge with fire and   if
you went there   your footprints would turn the desert sand

to glass shone in blue pools behind you   as you ran   lonely
says the limes mourn their thin branches   how they taper so
lovely into leaf   and the leaf mourns the white   louse that pierced

its under-skin   and the louse mourns the warm wind that carried it there
from another orchard   another country   where the field mice lean

each evening toward the distant town to let their brothers know
they remember   *what?*   lonely doesn't say   says only

an old desk drawer holds all the love of your life   says you
dream in ink and parchment   lonely says you punctuate your sleep

a rash of dashes and commas   release the warm wind of citrus
into air as though it were breath   lonely says   lonely   says
yes   there's another   yes   another longing   the breath of

breath   street of the street   the louse of the louse   and blue glass
moon reflected within the ocean it wants to become   beneath your feet

Unblurred

look at the shimmer of new ice upon the road   heartless
call it the slug's silver path   its thinning memory of where

and how   call it north   east   and south   call it dying rash stars
against the sky   a flame   a way thick and course
forget young trees lick spindly roots   love

suckled soil   so much the asphalt stretched   there to here
so much in coming and going   the way of us in the night

dark air   imagining his hand   *here*   or distance
from one another   the length of a rib   circumference of thigh   a navel

blind under the rasp   his name expelled   sigh
look how this shimmer   divides him in two   the passage from mouth

to heart   chest to belly   its rise and stall   the way from there to here
understand what loss   the road's simple route   conduit of our making
the muffled ignition   shallow sleep   a blazing trail

how simple could be his direction through this night   *here*
here   hands extended before him   my breast's easy braille

Keen

before me he loves that which he loves to which there is no end
there is the forest   within which is the dogwood and the contingent

blueberry bush breathing its piney hedge and crouch   the barn swallow
for which i cannot fault him   its swoop and milky curve   its watery eye
he loves the bread cooking in the kitchen   exhaling a yeasty bloom

into sunday's din   the car engine's   a hungry clause and eager carriage *away*
away   the street cleaner's regularity   its circuitous trajectory

the plane's painted belly   retreating above   and the guitar   her seductive curve
the easy nestle into his arm's crook   he loves the coffee grinder's narrow complaint

and the porn star's vacuous glare   not unlike the season's first diaphanous grape
its dim sugary musk   before me he loves that which he loves   to which there is no end

argument and rhetoric   their cruel task   enthymeme's deductive carriage *away*
away that refuses point   counter point   fruit and seed   bark and flower
the causal relationship of heat and wax   he opens his mouth to its ripening flourish

the syllable's tick and trip   its metered and ravenous note   though silence is a love
we both understand   its easy pace   its tenuous stay   the way even the room embraces

belly beak belly wing belly

moves toward the path of a train belly

takes a cab to midtown   belly buys

an umbrella in the rain   elegy for my

belly   for my belly that

cannot sing

Treaty

last night my chest opened like a house
swinging the front doors back on their hinges

the night found its way inside   curled into a backdrop
for the heart   which beat a strange and tangled rhythm
the ribs stood   rigidly futile   scaffolding my failures

my muscles   my tendons   my arteries and veins
and when the doors flew open   no herd of wildebeests

sprinted forward   no black mamba slithered   no zebras
darted from behind my lungs   no giraffes sauntered out

no meerkats   no mongoose   cheetahs nor gazelle
fleeing them   i felt my chest open on a hinge of night

inside i found muscle   tendons   arteries and veins
what there avowed what i am no more than what
i am not   do you hear the heart's struggle to beat again

do you hear the savanna's grasses   rattling the wind like a cage
the sound of those beasts grazing   each pace of feral plain

Secede

in the house next door   newlyweds die
slowly   into each other's arms

side by side on their newlywed sheets
their hands reach for universe after universe
through the glimmer of night they haul into their room

they sigh toward the north   wind rapping at their door
surrender their legs to the meringue of flies on the sill

they shut their eyes to the enchantment of grubs   buried deep
in the backyard soil   the garden languishing like a starlet

grown old   they cannot help but dream the fireplace
consumes them   in the house next door   newlyweds

try to remember the name of the wind that haunts
their halls   imagine it a nirvana that keeps
the milk's ripple   and lights the carrot's pith

the begonias littering the porch   typical in their waxy
way of fauna   tended by the most ordinary touch

Guile

as for the earth in the thick of summer   it forgets its song
the ground grows deeper   everyday   the sun seeks out

its furthest reaches while ants   single file   consume
each word we say   what of my face do you imagine keeping?
not even your eyes can resist this past   solitary damp

some radiant lust that vines the season you remember
how long ago   green carpeting   knees rubbed raw

light filtered into pink squares patterned
on the boarding room ceiling

my shoulder   and then my knee   your steeled breath
this yellow lawn confirms the earth's forgotten song

some radiant longing that raises every vein   first
your temple throbbing   year after year   then the forehead
its blue-pulsed release of some quieted need

oh but the earth's surrender to the sun's seared conviction
oh but the scorched grass   the relentless and prying heat

Revel

at your touch i swallow a creak of rusty hinge   i swallow
einstein's violin   they rub against each other like flecked wings

in my throat   expel the highest edge of air   or is it a step's squeak
a balloon raked by a comb   styrofoam against styrofoam   and then
a chorus of *oh*   one sound to the other   there exists no love

without a blue morning song   there exists no love without the trout's
body slapping water on a chill lake   without the slightest timbre

of breaking glass clearing the air into what afterwards is silence   there is
no love without love which is a sound   which is a tuba in an open field

which is water spray against window   which is the inner thud of your heart
your heart your heart   at my touch you swallow a creak of rusty hinge

you swallow a blue morning song without which there exists nothing of us
no breath nor quake   no shiver nor reach into the muscled crescendo of a car's
penetrating approach   the street outside   then its passing   without which

you grow silent   and in silence you breathe *a capella* into the evening grown
darker than grass   into the room which holds its own breath   waiting to hear

Vicarial

the flamingos across the street arc in anticipation of the world
granting them some kind of life   hover at the edge of a plastic

reconciliation with air   with sunlight and thunder   with god's green
field   an ocean thrashing at curve and clasp   they are
made by a man   who bends over each slight

beak   air-brushing life into its black silhouette
are made by a woman   who's left finger

grazes the white wisp of feather   a suggestion   wing and plume
god does not want their perch at the hedge   some dumb

blasphemy   every blink   we have ever had
the flamingos across the street are part of the lawn's september

send their half-precious silhouettes   blank as another st louis day   skirting
the drive-way where an eden   crests around a barbeque pit
where divinity is dewy   mulched   mowed each week   and cliffs

cut below a pink vortex   impossible clouds   setting sun   miter-
framed   a gold-leafed gild   squared on the living room wall

Sate

the fat dancers in the swimming pool
have learned   anything in water is beautiful

and so   in unison   swell their unlikely
movement   spin through atmosphere
that imagines them   the lightest of masses

 look at their suspended stomachs bob sway
the huge breasts   water's slow orbit as lap

currents would ripple a crane staked to her own
inevitable lift and soar   they   not unlike her   white

skull caps   arms spread wide as crane wings spread
landscape into passing canvass   the fat dancers

look   their suspended stomachs   worth
expands and floats   they gleam in the pool's
light   reflect the burden of slick presence

as the crane understands   lumber
gravity   the way a body rises in spite of itself

(third note)

it is the hour in which

i think of you

it is the hour in

which i think

of you it is the

hour in which

i think of you

Lark

the mouth appeared first on his rib like a fluttering navel
with teeth   it spoke incessantly   and could not be fed enough

it laughed when i touched him   it whispered under the sheets
ignited each tapestry of night with a love for the letter *t*:
tango   talpa   touch   tandem   when i put my lips to his back

it said *timbal*   when i kissed his stomach   it said *tick*   when i nudged
his cock with my chin   then my cheek   it breathed deeply into the crease

of his leg   breathed deeply the body's dream of death   it said *tropic*
trundle   tragus   tuft ... if it were not for that jet stream cutting the sky

i would forget him   his square shoulder   open jaw   his worried hands
even the mouth that appeared later on his chest   fluttering like a winged

beetle   when i kissed his neck   his clavicle   his head   it said *torn*
it said *trodden   tarnish   tumid   trance   turgent   trudge   tremble   trust*
i close my ears to its secrets   turned my eyes from its parted lips

at times   a still day dank with the macerations of autumn upturned   brings
his scent back to me   though the air unmoving and silent   does not sound true

Unloose

today they tell each other their dreams   his has an apocalypse
of the most spectacular sort   mountains collapsing into themselves

and the sky   a screen of fire   hers   more simple   a lost spaniel   a broken
wrench   walk through a narrow alley that leads to her home
but even in this dream   she is lost   her front door out of reach

around the next corner   or the next   or then never anywhere   so that
she moves with no direction but a thought   *to find*

she doesn't know what   the misplaced stamps   the telephone which rings
rings in the background   perhaps the child whose face blinks back

her own confusion   her home stands before her   but she seeks only
a moment to wake within   they tell each other their dreams   not because

they lack for epiphany   wait for revelation around the next corner   or the next
eventually   everywhere   the locusts speak their minds   mossed rocks
shrug to the concept of perpetual desire   mulch continues to placate

the broad feet of hemlock   every worry in the world could not add up to
the misfortune of forgetting   their eyes blind as oranges to   what's behind them

Wilt

perhaps desire arrives finally   frayed and trodden   say then   you
lower yourself onto him and the world splits in two   say the universe

blinks and facilitates your rocking with an absence of gravity
a levity in your limbs   your long vowels expended   as a trajectory that years
after the body's death   rides the sun's rogue flares   in this moment

he will mourn you as the quail's caw mourns her shattered eggs   as
the mimosa tree mourns dying light with its bristled orange blooms   as the river's

rush mourns the stone's lost yet stippled way   can you save more than this coming
into a heightened lift and sway   more than your shoulders slackened into his ribs

more   say   than even you can regret   will he falter   will he wonder when you finish
about his heart's scuffle   perhaps desire does arrive   begging his passage into your

room   his shirt torn   his hands   a cracked desert   longing   will you mourn
his lost way   will you hear the clink of a spoon in the kitchen as the day settles
onto the wide wave of your hip   think *butter starlight voyage gloom*

or does the consequent noon dictate   already   his silence   his absence   his departure
like an engine retreating into nighttime's distance   its domed punctured curve

(fourth note)

elegy now

for the grackle at the

edge of the road become

blue flutter instead

of death

Salacity

the cardinal is back   like a sentry stalking
the neighborhood   he understands

something of cruelty   withdraws each time
i lean too near   even though the glass
gives him back his own wounded stare

he has swallowed a berry   as blue as the earth   though
my room is what he wants   not the yield of sky

scraping dogwood   nor his own blazed reflection
against the orbed terrain of my face

hovered at the kitchen table   he senses me
but the room will not be his   the cardinal is back

he has eaten a berry as big as the world   and tries
to take what he pleases   he swallows sky
he devours a galaxy of lawn and hedge   and yet

beyond   the daytime moon is just   a lost plane
a clouded lid   a silent   unremarkable gape

Tautology

if you killed me now   my legs would walk to another country
happy for their journey away from the hips' locked carriage

my eyes would roll into glass   reflect first   all we have ever
mentioned   about the creeping westward blue   hovering above
my eyes   would roll   slowly   from my skull   into the green

tired of all they've seen   at the moment of my death   my body would
cascade into four thousand ripples   as though remembering the water

from which it came   remembering your hand   the vortices'
swirl of each imprint you made on me   waterfall and white foam

come together again   belly heave and fraction of each touch
if you killed me now   my face would become your face   brother

soldier   lawn-keeper   nurse   at this moment of my death   this moment
crisp with the smell of smoke that circles autumn   know this   the red
scarf tied around the head of the old woman at the bus stop   me   her

hands   her clenched jaw   me   and within her   an animal outline   deltoid curve
soft sagging flesh   an animal fanged within   her perfect folds

Cede

in your sleep you turn a thousand revolutions
away from me   your chest rises first

into the brindled calligraphy of branches
cast on the lamp shade   which then recedes into the bed's
plush blindness   i fail here   where your breath

translates the room's exhalation   where the glint
of the neighbor's light going out snuffs your form

into the moon's silver line   i cannot find you   have lost
our beginning   your head becomes the streetlight's

knobby tip   your arm the mulberry's bitten branch
in your sleep you turn toward the end i cannot see

not a calligraphy of branches   but a tree unearthed
and transposed   its roots turned up   its leaves meeting
finally the grass   with whom it could share a voice

then wind without which   the leaves fall voiceless   *hush*
hush   as the night   within which   these forms are useless

Scope

the smallest animals with the smallest feet   each
feel a death descend like a fleet shadow   that may be a cloud

come over the sun   or a branch shifted   or a change of day   but mostly
indicates a great hunger in the woods   an insatiable lust in the alders
a voracious intent of flight that seems   itself to turn the leaves

to silvered sides   as if in warning   the red tail hawk   unappeasable
glides   a long lawn   the thick growth stalks the rape that mounts

the hemlock   slowly   lifts   falls on wind   the same slow rhythm
afternoon   sweet murderer   feathered scythe   hooked cataclysm

ruthless   taloned deluge   disaster blessed indifferent   a devastation of air
and flight   what stalks the smallest animals   with the smallest hearts

shrieks   its long shadow over sun   allows an unappeasable
constant gnaw   perhaps as much
from kill as   the killed   perhaps as much from bone crack

as from meat   this morning   two jays joust a nearby elm   all
wing   flail the ground littered with berries   for which they vie

Design

i will not write you an elegy
big-mouthed woman   whose breasts

hugged the microphone stand   some hugged breadfruit dream
nippled clouds   woman whose arms winged softly
her armpits   billowing   flourish skin   bounty

thighs and ass enveloping the world
musked sweat   satin teeth

tunneled through   closets of angels
their gild garments

your eyes blink back salty foam
i will not write you   an elegy

though your voice encompasses   the world
raspy under-song   glare
c-notes crowning you   each time you walk   on stage

listen to the cardinal cutting a racket through my neighbor's pine
hear his salutation   his winged confirmation   music   un-stilled

Batten

believe me   the hydrangea hangs its head low   not because the sun
in another hemisphere   evades the cool hills   the white stucco houses there

slanted against bright   so each blocks light against   the horizon
not because the soil seethes   sweet excrement of earthworms
who eat the lives we discard   and so love us most of all   believe that

between the green blades   long mouth of iris   above flayed
legs   onion flocking the base of the lilac   death wraps around

hummed grass   around green   toothed
smell of season   just so

heavier each day into summer   how   can the hydrangea do anything else
but light itself into pinks   creams   how can it not hang   head low

worry the green blades   the long mouth   iris swathed purple
death ache   when it is new   and smells like spring   what carcass
brings   a waft twist   collapses   into air   reminds us we are each

heading back   to earth   the smell of us lifted   gentle rot
in the palm   sugar blossom   the lilt   a crippled goodbye

Hover

it's only a matter of time after you speak of the garden   and the wood
that conversation turns to the snake   yes   that snake   he was

after all   the star-draw   the brando   the de niro   the sweaty
t shirt   the half burnt pall mall   perched in the corner of that sweet
mouth   he was king of the show   he was a three ring circus

tumbled into town   a velvet painting so plush   your hand
reaches out to touch   before you know what you want

he was no 50-cent theatre with sticky floors   a torn screen   he
was a slap on the ass i tell you   he   was a party waiting to happen

so if one small girl   imagines herself to be the bergman in casa blanca
it's only a matter of time before it happens   her lips big as a man's

body   perfectly lined   a red velvet bow so plush   they await a kiss that will
never come   isn't there always a scene with a snake   leaning in her doorway
when she arrives home   opening the cab door   tossing a coin in the air as he leans

his padded shoulder against her building   poor girl   standing there   the plane
flies away   skirt wind-whipped   her lips hungering what they miss

Pallor

the way of hunger   is the only   way
the way that it lunges   breathes   but

only after
it sits   patient in the dark
calmly observes   your small movements

the way your left hand
strokes the back   of your right hand

the puckered corner   of your mouth
turned   around the hemisphere of longing

which has become   the country you dream of leaving
the way of hunger is   the way

of your left hand   the hand of hurricanes and
lightening   the hand of creosote   pungent
in the heated desert morning

creosote waits also   rain released   sun's small movement
slow   turn of the world come to unleash   that scented fury

Cloy

watch without end   these women in the pond   their slick
animal limbs fanned   against water surface   hair matted fur

the strong   swell of their necks   shoulders   lurching first forward
then back   each body determines a lithe moment   balances the new lift
chill   currents   both small and grand

flare   the bow of the sternum   curve of the back as arms   butterfly against
their ribbed sides   resembling great figureheads   at the prow of a ship

cut paths through breaks   in front of them   skirt water over
breasts   an explosion of limbs   re-surfaced   balmy upstate air

divulging   battering   sorrow that resists the tar streaked afternoon
the city   hours from here   watch   calamity for this   long   as if it were

forthright   as simple   a bowed rib cage   a curved spine   stretch
of forearm into what surely   is a stout moment of reckoning   an afternoon's
disregard   denial of what happens beyond   the water's edge   beyond buoyancy

and the angular truth of   ankle   knee   or elbow   flailing each axis by which
the body ascends   each hinge of the lung's labor   heart's brawl

Fete

i am last in line at the coffee shop bathroom   where the woman ahead
is a brisk gust   a flutter   a skirt swelled at the knees   who turns a grin

through the narrow space   turns her eyes through that narrow space
and we meet   at the door's eclipse   at the door's shudder   at the door's
decreasing line of light   and i love her   in this moment   imagine

the skirt lifting   its green trail   her gentle squat   her eyes fixed forward on
muraled walls   the empty picture frame above the sink   i am afraid she is too

easy to love   and begin again   see a small breath exhaled at the moment her body's
water lets go   lips pursed to blow a candle   to clear the dust from a photo

her breasts un-raised   shoulders slumped   lips pursed to kiss   and kiss again
in the same way they would push air out   or draw it in   i am last in line

to her solitude   the skirt lifting   her hips' suspended squat   the echoed trickle
that reminds her   a beach and a whistle   long grass   highway's buzz
her way home   diesel smell and salt   she leaves with the same   flourish

let her let her pass   ebb down the long   stairwell   under the just soaked
fern   uncoiling its breezy wants   whispers: *love   let her go . . .*

Odium

the bitterness of this fruit   feeds a deeper   want
ferns fray detail from the lowest   edged   forest

hand-winged bats bite outlines   of flies
the wind   *oooohs* itself   out of existence   thinning
into one thought   this apple descends   dulled

memory of tart   rooted there   the mind's wide
prairie   swayed by dying wind   shadowed bat

forest   sycamore feet   by a light
green   undoing   the world cannot be more

try to wish the sky   fuller   the apple   less ripe
the bitterness of this fruit   feeds deeper want

memory rooted   in thatch and weave
the tedium of peel   and core   the logic of stem
even the flies descend   against the bats aerial   hunger

their own feast   their carrion dream of elbow   claw
maggoted gnaw to bone   their plump readying

Desist

to dream of dark brown honey means   the cumulus sky has not yet
descended upon   your bed   means the cows in their wisdom   retreat

to a distant field   the smell of lightening   the hooved earth
beneath them means   the snakes near the pond   cross jutting rocks
pocked yellow moss   dream your hands clasp together   implies

the basil comes to flower   a diagram of bees   swarming quick
desire   each purple bloom suggests   the spring will circle coolly

about your fingers   to abandon your fear of cliffs   indicates your
moment of understanding   the grieved heaviness of stone fruits

derelict on the branch   cherries scorned by heat   peaches hollowed rot
plums   wormy and reamed through   dark brown honey means

your mouth   a speckled harvest   your mouth   a diagram of bees swarmed
the tender of my breast   your mouth   dew damp   sting
the hind wing   folding slightly   the abdomen curls   the wax glands pull up

and for venom's clear shot   my throat   closing slowly around this
swelling   mind reeling   bustle long   lost breath

(the fifth note)

elegy for what becomes

shhhhhhhhhhhhhhhhhhhhhhhhhhhhhh

the cab ride

home

Ebb

the earth is about to fail   fall onto winter knees
but first   the couple that lives next door   will burn leaves

in the back yard   sheath themselves   knotty plaid
pretend their lives full   with landscaping   then
after dinner out   the waiter notices her fawn eyes

looks   at her hands reaching for bread   her husband
notices   does not look up   does not challenge him

it feels good to know   his wife is wanted   when he lays
next to her   he will lay with smoke from the fire   the waiter's

eyes   the warm smell of yeast   fresh baked bread
the earth is about to fail   and he welcomes it   waits for grass

withered   looks long at his wife's hands   reach for a cover
she will pull up against her   though   chill already comes
as if no   warmth she can find in him   across town   the waiter

has already forgotten   counts his change   laughs with the cook   at
the kitchen door   his visible breath   billows upward   escapes him

Vice

a tall chestnut has forsaken the forest   has fallen onto its side
forlorn   hopelessly abandoning   its green posture

could no longer stand   could not endure   one more night
bugs skimming its tip   stars forever out of reach   it could not
allow   one more day to pass without lying down   luxury

prostrate in grass   to the thicket's edge   a chain saw now
intrudes the calm   honeysuckle   mullein   rips away hollow

revs' teeth   the tree   supine surrender   chewing first branch
branch   then trunk   broken   the smallest

cross sections   a century   how brave this great   renunciation
height   a single tree forsaking   what we hold dear   the whole

the clutch   to lie down on its side   prostrate   a soft compendium
bark leaving now   a window in the thick overgrowth   which reveals
each car's arrival   each passerby   this man   who walks the road   who pauses

at the woods' grim opening   stopping to see his own reflection
startled conflict   the stark image he doesn't understand   the tree imagined

43

Cupidity

in one cut   this peach will give up   a blood red center
a spiked underneath   the pit in fleshy tendrils   dimpled

center   the hard constant to   being whatever
being a bled open sea   for sky   and cloud
that torch the corners of morning   fleet fire

as you tick minutes   your voice
strumming   the low octave just before

growl   just before hum   the jagged trickle
dislodged   set free   brief capture   not unlike

a perch unhooked   its rippled fire   orange stripes
over scales   over gills which give up   a blood red center

unwillingly   gape the hard accordion   being   constant and not
the heave up   and back against air not water   suffocated
want want want   with each flail   for water   breath

i hear   you call my name sometimes   and i think   you are mine
linger   with my knife poised   edged at the skin   wait for it to give

Muster

on a night like this pity   the elegant universe brimming   its transparent
beasts   its constellations flat-backed   their poor crooked shoulders

sodden claws   how lonely the invisible orbits   etched in space
voiceless spackle   distantly   with stars that die their long   luminous
deaths   i'm watching this night   these beautiful deaths   a window

on this side of which   a cluster of bodies dances   11 pm   swinging arms
their heads in the deepest   glee   their ligaments and bones

their rounded skulls   their flash pan   gleaming eyes   dancing
a momentary stay   their own stark failings   the lung-shudder stillness

the silenced heart   they sweat their humid   dreams against each hip
and hip   as forever   on a night like this   pity   them too

a cluster of faith   their transitory limbs   their swinging arms   flexed necks
their charming thighs carrying them   across a wood floor   nailed down before
they were born   which remains after their stunning faces'

own departures   through the dark   windows behind them
the scum-covered lake   sits stagnant   with each   black reflection

Laud

he approaches a hill that rises   an impossible   point   a studio
follows a road dying into sky   the sky a boundary   never reached

he pedals the thick   thighs drag backward
as his mind slips   the morning's faint sheets   light barely
with him   her   he imagines   sour breath   raised ribs

her leg thrown free   five other people in the room   i pedal next
to him   pumped legs   the instructor's   *push   push   push*

push   push   push   i hear he heaves   hard   stands
into it   raises his spine   in dog bristled midnight

now he leans his forehead to the towel   as though to gently kiss the face
of her   or nudge an ear   approaches the hill   as though   she is under

his flared chest   tapered swell   a blood rush   her leg thrown
around him   over his back   pulling him down the hill's   resistance
tugging him against   the road's curve   the rise   fall of his shoulders

riding as she would press   pull   the room absent of us   as we imagine
what crests   our collapse   peaks the inward horizon   push toward

Strafe

the seats in the club   not leather   not cloth   a thing as brown
her snug cigarette grip   smoke   a television-

light behind   a bar where the world cup   plays a wide
green field   he sees   yet cannot comprehend   the players' muscled
legs   soaked sweat jerseys   the crowd pulsing each goal

at home his wife   sleeps in a cotton nightie   clouds printed into
blue sky   what he imagines blue sky   an endless blue fleeced

over her pendulous breasts   rounded belly   though this woman
at the bar   is not his wife   her hair does not smell   like trees

peppermint   her lips purse   in expectation   her brows point toward
the door   the seats   at the bar   not the oatmeal upholstery of chairs

in his home   where his wife sleeps   soundly   in a flock of clouds that take her
to nether space   in a dream of   the high clock over   London   as it rings
as rain beats down   as her dream umbrella wets   her dream shoes   and soaks

the patter of his absence   against   her wide dream face   her sky
eyes clenched   closed   rhythm she makes   as somewhere to go

Promiscuity

tell me this autumn day   in each way   the same as yesterday
golfers walk   their yellow course   cars passing   divide us in two

i don't like the taste of honey   any more this morning   than last night
the month   origami minute   folded into hour   week   the crease
of his neck as he turns to see   night billow open   its sheets tell me

i am bored with this   lovely life   these lewd trees offer themselves
the same gold abundance   their last thirst   left them

to sky   who bares herself black   smooth   a lover's bite
each way the same as yesterday   the sky   she cups   in dark palms

unmakes   her dark breath   as moving leaves
as golfers watch   her rear away   pink   stay their course

i am bored with this lovely   life   and do not know   the names of these trees
i call them   *sugar   darling   charming   sweet   lovely   handsome   love*
dear   the sun and sky gold   tongued   a warm shimmer

a want   a lure going   the easy   orbit of the world
a want   a lure going   the easy   orbit of the world

Apt

the world still   within his voice   the static character   of my name
on his tongue   what form   what worship comes from desire   does it

speak the room   the desk   the windows that shed barely any
light   the books that line the walls   the floor that resists his every step
this morning   three women stood   at the bakery counter   surveying

treats   glass   a still fascination   heavy pause
gave way eventually   their evocative devotions   *cruller*

éclair   long-john   tart   sweet idolatry   tonight
my own worship of stars   bees   dogs   a worship of stones

fish and shit   carcass and fire   grass cascading down a s lope   the skeletons
of every animal anchors them   how still the world we find   barely

spoken   the heavy pause   afternoon disappearing   the gray envelope of evening
or the far whine of a freeway   its constant labor   removal and delivery
my name   has a longing all its own   to be fawned over   to have the vowel

stretched   bent   settle into the soft fricative release   the single syllable
suspended   vacillated   expelled finally   breathless   hesitant refusal

Gather

near me   nothing but distances   cars far away   the long drawn
sound   the interstate and city   then its trains ever   slowly

arriving   lights   haloed with exhaust haze   we   from very
far away   see this populous   the tall buildings   the blinking
arches and   think it beautiful   the pissed-in alleys   the loaded dumpsters

we call home   the science of departure   how amongst these
thousand hills   we postulate outcome   measure components

trace median pathways   a destination proved against   all other
possibilities   what fraction of yearning quantifies   desire

we multiply it by the miles   from you to me   if i were to leave this chair
come to you   wind's speed   nothing but distance between us

and you traveled toward   your first compulsion   science
assumes we will never   find our way to   the place of origin
by what axiom   do we determine the road   accommodate our

city grids   its distance   the roads   cornered against each other
the buses loaded   expectation   each face   passage yet realized

Crevice

she dreams   a lion rises in her chest   waits for the first   clattered rustle
of morning to pounce and   roar   so she will not wake   do you see

she will not wake   she falls deeper into   her city of sleep
walks the concrete   paths of her refusal   the dark alleys of her will
watches the stoplight   she imagines   *blink blink* her cautions into

the earliest plum dawn   she understands the blacktop   has no memory of grass
the red car whirring past   spins a story of its own   the interstate in the distance

if given a chance   will devour this woman   never mind the tin articles   of the city
tires that run   back windows   never mind the boy   the bullet taste

runs him down   into the city's drains   passes through him
lodges still in its asphalt face   she dreams a lion wakes in her

ravenous   it has no memory of shot   nor the quiet hum   evening news balanced
above the neighborhood   it will eat a boy whole   hungers eclipse
swiftly   not even the streetlights remember   a ravaged thing

the failing axis of   her home   anticipates the purple outline   of a shrill
woman's wail   far off   even the sluggish sun grips   these grieving hills

Twain

the last time i tried   to ride a horse i bleated   a fear
my cousin lifted me toward her   the horse

spooked and ran away   without me   her black eyes
turned in their sockets   watched me into the leafy   background
she retreats   the moment came   went   and went again

i see her run away   imagine her filled   with glass eyes
that bob against her sides   as she runs   all of them

looking toward   my backward direction   the beige grasses
flattened   her ears swayed   her liquid mane

my cousin held my waist   tightly   his chaffed hands   my legs
bent upward   stirrup ready   the horse against my fear

then   to watch her run away   i see her run away
i see her look   wildly into my eyes   the slow
revolution   my youth begins to spin   faster   faster   she

sees my moon-faced revelation   i am a burden   i am a burden
and her back   its velvet spirals   cannot hold me

Sunder

listen to the flock   grackles praising the just   softening
fig   the disturbed hush   brushed back   their wings

the placid spiral   their hovered beaks   bleating
a steel gravity   say the tree   say the fig's altar
say the mute sugar invoking   seeds   dark skin

purpled from green   say a woman whose eyes
close   against clawed and feathered descent

a brutal harvesting   a hewn heart   the fricative
branches craggy   their upward reach   say here

a bird   an animal receives   a feathered happening
listens to the flocked   emergence   in its throat

a woman   whose brown eyes bloom   inward
the fig's implosive   ripening   or
assumption billowed   a velvet robe

here   her mouth   opens like a fig
listen to plum   valediction   confess to be yours

Hush

forgive the tea for not   keeping you here   this moment
allowing you   to wander past the open   tables

the café door   the woman limping in now
the scent of   gardenia she brings   settles on your shoulders
but cannot keep you   your left ankle feels the pace

an ant   forgive this ant   his legions of busy intent
cannot know   gardenia or   the woman's small agonies

or the tea disappointing   its bitter tongue   forgive your tongue
that knows nothing   but want   cannot understand a siren   wailing

the window   or the disappearing earth   or the perfect
taste of desolation   in his mouth   forgive his mouth   its untold velocities

its woody intent   its yearning to be   unfastened   from the world
you might unbutton a button   or pull back the collar   of a stiff linen
blouse   imagine   this blouse   freshly ironed   warm to the touch   it smells

lightly of bleach   air   when you lift it   bring it to the bed   lay it there
see it without your form   flat   lifeless as if   you are already gone

Parse

i am waiting for wind   i am waiting for   grass to move air
to find life   for the squirrel there   to brace itself   an imagined death

its fur ripples for water   to wave the pool's side   i am waiting for
the hopeless pinecones   to nudge their boughs   the dirt road
a rolled gust   some ache   a life and rotation   for clouds to find their pace

a great white herd of bison   slowly   crossing the sky   thunder
cracks   their hoof-beats first   a vertical downpour   then lightening

then the sound of soft   vaporous migration   new satin shoes
or a red bicycle   lying lazily on its side   the rider wades   pant cuffs turned

a slippery chill   stream dressed dull   lichen green
i am waiting for   the wind to pass   a barreling truck   for it to descend

this calm   a great dying breath   crossing the plains   stretched westward
these low hills   right to your doorstep   right to the home where   you pack this life
into small boxes   sent further and further away from me   outside

afternoon soaks lawn   rubs its grey flank   the undefeated pines   each
understand   gravity buckles   pulls back to earth   what longs to drift away

Verve

the man who left his wife   for a lilac bush   was not a questioning man
he hummed   devotions at day break   as anyone would   who'd seen sun's

furious crest   seer the eastern ridge red   he composed letters
of hard bread   his dreams   like the rest of us   closed   his eyes
as flecked black flight   starlings in fear they might   lose their way

his wife   how   handsome   her adobe skin   her forest of hair   resistant
to the ways   wind longs to overcome   unlike the lilac

that moves fitfully   here   there   bobs plum clusters   an invisible
fury   gusts waves capacious scent   a sexual cascade   crushing

loveliness   but most flaunts willingness   to bend   to surrender whispers
its loquacious rustling   leaves   the man who left   for a lilac bush   understood

the nature   of losing one's way   his wife   the tapered apex of each finger
could not feel soil   surge life   the soft wood he understood   that her ears
deafened to the botanical call   pollen etched   the air measured   syllables

lilac   sweet flock   florid rash   violet effusion   most lascivious shrub—
how disloyal   bawdy sway   how ornate   boughs   of swelled blooms

Trove

outside   a man kneels in my front yard   scooping dirt into a zip- lock bag
he fingers   molding rose   takes a leaf   two circles   the spent lilac

i leave the house to meet him   excuse his trespass which   he thanks
he brushes the lilac's sway   his flat palm   the way you would muss
the hair of a boy   rub the shoulders of a sallow   friend   slowly wave goodbye

the lilac   his mother's   who died last week   who kneeled thirty-two years ago
here   or just a moment ago   spade perhaps in hand   wind articulating trees'

movement   though a new sound   and the air's wet breath   of grass
a new smell   and the earth's musk emulsion   death on her hands

the scent of her son   emerged from   the birth of trees   across the street
the son   who   on his way inside   reaches to her where   she kneels   scooping dirt

a hole widening   thirty-two years later   he possibly understands now   her task
explains her ashes to me   who now lives in her home   and when she
takes his hands   to steady her rise   and they stand   face to face   eye to eye

like lovers   breath   seamless   touching sternums   braced
the muffled   rhythm of bright fracture   beat in them both

Lurk

open your mouth   to a whisper that   escapes the soft oval within you
the small harp   in your throat   thin vibration   of your lungs strung tight

your mouth around it   understands vacuous   space
understands the glacier's blue repose   the horse's gleaming flank
underbelly of its diction   the soft pile   its back swelling open

air   an expanding whisper   vapor expelled   a gully's mist   body
ballooned   dashed cliffs in return   echo back   low

seduction   a landscape fails only   because it does not know   your name
your curved calf   does not hold your footprints   its muddy palms   we

remain like this   you and I   hobbled in quietude   you can open
your mouth to desert dunes   moved by wind   indifferent to the smallest

thing that breathes there   a whisper   a violet evening   in near   silence
swallows frigid corners   a widening warmth expressed   deep within
a heat taken up   by the heart's task to quake   thunder and blood

your veined words   realize the dream   pulsed rhythm in your wrists —
the way the body   wants for syllable   actuates our tranquil grammar

LOVELY GUN

Of Me You Quit Saying So

I never turn toward the camera
Though I watch the news

How close we would be Touching the other country
A trigger love

Talk about static If you convince
The sea into having us
Static is no matter

My face not turned toward you
My ear not at your throat which says *not again*

Gospeling

You shake a mile of ocean
not your shoulders but a different language

Maybe you're talking in your sleep
When I am watching the Ethiopian grocer
hand me change

Quiet is one language of war but
Most importantly only one

Cartographilia

The door doesn't understand solitude anymore than you
having always sought or been sought

I mean to say I know less and less
And know you know less and less also

The shore edge foam and caw of water
You lose

I do not know what the air says to you
The closet with your shoes is quiet like the door

Instead of knowing You sleep somewhere else
You feel the air preparing to speak

Forms of Range and Loathing

typical of an arid country among hundreds of other flora
you find half a province of avalanches

parts are desert

I might say light defeated by a dark thing that strips
mountain and bullet

                  no

the mountains have forgotten airborne
you would never say howl
never say mountain

or region or enemy
you say men's mouths are the woods' black holes

I'm thinking The guy on TV didn't seem upset about
killing his wife If he'd done so but he didn't he says

nothing about him if not after an interview
tuft bodies of red wings scatter the lawns

did you hear
birds out of sky
some dead wind

he didn't seem upset and so may as well
have killed his wife
a jury says

If you could hear me now I'm not sure how important
it might seem In another language

Hope is not too much or that a random crime
might mean We share something

Lost Private

In Harlem people push baby carriages around
You read this somewhere

If I were to drive as far as land becomes
Other land

Nowhere do I hear you say So what
When the dog is out

the door open to dark shiver
and night not sure where to go

Home will be something like this
The door stays the same

Mission

So many are missing
And call for their arms to walk the hundred miles

The white torch skimming the way a body ignites
An arm feels the ground beneath it

The waking helps no gunshot
The skull understands no loss

The boy is wearing a striped shirt dark blue
His hair grown over his ears

The flash lights
knuckled orange rounds

Recruit

Tell her to go home Tell her a road and a car
Are two different things in two different places

When you think of her you think of yellow

Her nose breaks breath knowing
the head's solitude

her hip can hear you but not respond
which means her spine is dumb and gray
teeth and dust everywhere

tell her dust cares more than we do

Honor

Since the last storm
And roofs ripped away

The wind like that
careless

I have begun to imagine
    How a body peels away from itself

November Somewhere

No one has thought absence assembles hands
back from pieces

despite how cold it is everywhere
north of the equator

Your skies not Provenance nor hesitation
Whose bright teeth break calm

Because You Are Sleeping You Hold Your Gun

I won't tell you about the starlet Who's finally said
She'll have more children

74% disagree

The static sounds like A song about logistic metals
Your voice 16 lives ago

Keep her safe in your hand
Boom and Snap everywhere the street has flame

The descent stays Close your eyes
Give the children candy
They will love you

If The Sky Stays Quiet

On the 4th of July
We lit fires

The porches on fire
The sky on fire
The road on fire
The night on fire

bullets
everyone thought
were happy ghosts who remembered
nothing

The happy ghosts left in pick-up trucks
and sometimes on foot
sometimes

as a boy with a striped shirt blue waving
a miniature flag

The most wonderful thing About
Fire and living

The way my footsteps left in mud might
Outlast me

The red gone glow as afterward silence

Miles Where Forgotten Home

You will always look at the garden
And imagine

      a sternum
laced through with Allium roots

      that climate flower

      The same sun
beat sky

Last Week

I wanted sparkle to leave the metaphor behind

all sting my throat would have

light and greed
stubble
maybe

spit
liquor
a bed blanket smell

Not clean
some kind of filth in

Music thrashed My hair Your
hands brute hands

some jealous guy
watching

Satellite Dream

The back of your head
Your legs

I'm not able to put you all together
Like a broke down car

crash—
[the ground mentions]

here

The Lies I Want You To Tell Me

You come back through an open window
A curtain trailing wind in some
Movie about guns and war

       You are never thirsty which I say
I come to understand
But can't

You are not sleeping in a desert

       I can pack a house in St. Louis and shoulder it
Then appeasing some location
River or ledge

       A place begins here
       The curtains white

ruffled the way You'd imagine
       a home not in St. Louis
       but in Atlanta to have curtains

Drifting through an open Window like that

The window always belongs to a bedroom
Outside the bedroom is always a tree

You will tell me where she's going
You will tell the girl sneaks out of her room
You will tell when she comes back

Calligraphy

First of all
          no one will write

Letters reverse themselves little
letters

like an aleph or penmanship
or The Borges story which is now a video

Letters as big as Mountains is someone's religion
a rabbi hums his breath and means it so

I'll say the book reads back Of course mountain

mountain mountain Just as mountain cannot stop
being every gun in every country
Everywhere You are

Decide when to loop the O at the top
then practice what to say—

O Lovely

pavement and tar
No

candlesticks and holidays
orchard fruit

feel your pulse lipped
not longing

sweet

now
burn fills the air

A Parade Cannot Be Silent

Everyone seems excited by the new legislation
The snow forgotten forecast this morning

Grass still hunches in the doused fire of fall
Trees almost imagine

Can you recall any of this
I could write the chill wafts lonely

I could turn off the TV
But they're talking about something again

The weather Not the same pitched brawl
Every station says so

Do you remember that I hate raisins
In cookies

They seem forgotten both before and after
How then we know we miss something

No
We can talk about July beginning
The grass blanket

We watch the evening
Sprint and spray

Wake exhales
The other cot breathing

More clearly today
an ape at a European zoo Unexpectedly had a baby
Then in Chicago A wall folds around four firemen

The bricks had the conscience of bullets
A whispered disobedience

Miss the red eclipse Forget
I've told you about things you don't have

Sun Gospel

Also Gospel sun
And blinds wooden length

Not one part of me is in California

Everyone wanted California instead of
=== whatever they call it these days

There is a way you don't want to talk of
Sun Ra and the Whitney museum

And a way you do Regardless of   *who*
You belong to

what you'd say
I've forgotten

How Hills Collapse

A Volvo waved at me while I stood on a street Corner
at a cross walk as though to say

Hello or *Welcome* which also means
You don't belong

Which is right if right is something you know

I do not belong to the curb
or any sky behind me

or to gunfire begun and ended today
Which then

begins and ends tomorrow
not like a circle which neither begins nor ends

In the car the skeleton smiles

She was beautiful in the way a smiling woman
Disarms you so that her face is then a palm frond

Or a feather
Or something that moves in a way of falling when
The ground calls

you can hardly
imagine she is a skeleton inside
or patella femur and jaw

Except a lovely thing
To find something just and warm—

I've said this to the wall when I need
Your face there

But like the car
          I did not belong to the moment either
Not any understanding What a moment means

What color a moment could
Ever imagine

Whether blue is a possible luxury
Or light breaking away at the end of the day

Must always be romantic
Or if Romantic ever wanted to be red

Red has no allegiance
Red belongs to no one.

As Her arms did not belong to the steering wheel
Her shoulders to her arms

How Incredible You would think
her passing

Her hands whole
and intact

If Then Was Somehow Sorry for What it Had Been

Here's the thing I need to tell you
I curled up in a tight ball while they kicked me

I wore a sweater striped blue
a barber shop I remember her dad owned

nothing imagines itself this way

if nothing one day becomes a vowel and
speaking

it would follow to stammer
I wouldn't tell a perfect stranger

long ago what I wanted to give you
or have you give
            you
could not

Another Letter Midnight Writes

Imagine this flourish An overwrought purple
breath No not purple

I want You to ignite something
other than fire

So imagine I'd say a cat
no
A horse which is majestic in the way of things

too common though in television and stories
Kids singing you can't hold either

or some other beneath or above
Stop praying

I plug my ears to find out whether
A sound is outside of me or within

Consider rust and how the feel of it
Means a thing to do on any Saturday

An iris webbed of course The way purple
Would easily live within such circuits

The curled lips Or a wet tongue Spilling
a yellow blink as Yellow does in a wet morning

Opened within purple beating Not flowers

Of the heart Always impossible To not
come back That we come to a heart

Maybe a spin From Mountains
or home or the book you mean to read

forget I am trying to lead you to something
gleaned

Say you want
The bare chance of it

Can you find an earthquake of trees A moving chest
However beneath the ventricle sewn to itself

Not yet to itself And so yes I give up

Flourish you must say please that blood opens also
The way a breath leaves a body

only an eye milk glazed so Sight
won't have any starry offer

keep orange to yourself like this
go ahead And clouds also

Keep
the beautiful thing with not anything you agree

a chest in parts saying *goodbye whole thing*
goodbye what waking could have considered

though blinds open in morning say sun
more white and liquid

Don't say gray The way gray waits for him
a warm body His name was *that boy no one saw*

not Explosion Of course I've said what you say
the ear won't have

Which is not a theory of elephants bleating
Remembered

Or any wild thing Escaping

The sound goes by
A blue boy

why soaked red and torn

Say cigarettes and a lawn And A flourish

I've said this Flourish not met
Stop holding anything but bright

When life a body frees

Stop saying the eyes can't watch
how the soul lifts and flutters

Withstanding All the Days Again

I want to give you blazed
Balconies of some
Stucco city

Or barn bleached

Sun skipping rocks
To the sea

Someone sleeps
Just into the shade

imagine
His breathing inside

Write this to me

A Gun Retold the Lyric Way

The tenor Everyone talks She says
she makes a film about the soldier he was

The premier is sold out The way his story is told
We want everything that is here

I don't know my own parents either We often
begin with the option And the matter of

But has she looked up Tiberian?
Has the thing been

Part instruction

everything we want is here
it takes time it takes patience

It's a harsh Hush
image and story

Never take for granted someone pays
Most often someone says
A price

they pay
We love How much we know

A Closed Course

One last thing everyone says
Every day

Whether someone speaks to
Them or not

Everyone says one last thing before sleeping
Even alone

Perhaps though
No one said anything

a branch broke
then a screech comes from the trees

or
listening to an average voice

she remembers
difference desegregating the woods

The way metal doesn't make everyone
happy

or the taste of it
electric

Summit

a pen each morning Ties the laces of a shoe not dust
not boot

The window says quietly so as not to draw attention
Who eats rock   Who breathes flint

The boy wears a blue shirt Dark and striped
He brings a gun
a sun

Someone write this down

Narrative

I've decided to figure out How
You do not everyday
Think of a tank Not a horse arriving

In the very same way Say
a witness means to speak saving
Pages and pages

How does a tent smell
Does he talk in his sleep next to you
Do you know where he comes from

Does he also drink coffee
Do you notice feet not worn or dusty

If you close your eyes
A waterfall seems closer

Manuscript paper clips might be
Another thing common here and there

You should love anyone who
Bandages you

I understand what you'll miss
a smell won't be there

Here's what they call A story turned viral:
a great-horned owl swooped down on an 8 lb dog

after the news we celebrate
we line up our coolers and laugh

I think the bike disagreed With the direction
I was going so I fall
Which is what you remember

You've been here too The white tunnels
how fast the fence goes by

too simply said
and the wrong way to say it

you ask don't tell me Please
more than once

An Economy of Bullets Has More Sway

Bananas He bought tangerines or
He sold them

It happened before the book was written
But only talked about after

You wouldn't want to know this
If you were here and less
Mattered
     Stars
Rap rap rapping
No
the explosive kind
gunfired volumes
out of trees

I'm trying to tell you This book
The plot I've read didn't make sense

She would never have Had to choose
bananas or Tangerines which is the whole story

Why talk about things like this or Consider apples
Also as part of what she chooses

The story happens over and over
despite how I say
   You

Every Midnight is Where We Live

Hating the sun comes naturally
a bullet undoes A yellow flag
a stoplight red heartbeat

What someone may say under any other
Circumstances

You wouldn't say
I wonder how the sun has not left

You would remember grass differently
undone

maybe typical in the way of things
like the club closes at 2 really but 1:30 they stop you

Try stepping out like that
No where to go

A Tiger in Her Hands

A woman walks rooftops with
Swords and music

You might say the tune was catchy We've
caught her ache

I would say She is what anyone can only call
black hair trailing

or say
loneliness hates her

Counting by Fives and Grammar

When you say value you mean
you and I are conjugations

You would not name the color of the floor
        The floor then is just one word

I say dumb things
For example there are no such things as angels

       as handsome as they would be

Even the sentence might be blue again and again striped frost
       I am not lying to you about where we'll sleep

or what covers will be stitched and sound

To make a place Can be less than
Price to cash flow

You can read about merger But
it happens without you

O
the lung will become the shallow and the wall
will become the night

color let's say green crests maybe violet and then coast
cannot stop your absence either

you weigh and measure
          the migration of speech and name
          You also mean

When sky
          When the ground slips away

Trust Me is Only Pretending

Hello the monkeys say in a post card

Who sends this? Even if the greeting
Is well written

A monkey dressed in a pink dress Or a hat
is still a monkey

you are right to be embarrassed
That I need to say so

Looking fine is always A way
We stay fly – check me out

Shoes that shine Are black
Offset the part You don't like so much
My hips still move like that

No offense but it doesn't matter
You're lonely

You live in the way I speak back

What can you do about it When you forget
The boring stuff Managing is like that

The heartbeat earns more than it spends
There is no such thing as home

No Matter How the Water Means

How many look for the river they can smell
From very far away

Months have passed All afternoon
days off are any days more than one

Illuminate
I would say if I were a French boy dead and in love

which we remember as awnings
lit above bridges

you know water means no sound
              splitting a night is sweet or longed for
His feet are bare and you keep them in sight

a boy wearing a striped shirt
              you think not meaning to remember parts

refuse water
and walking

rivers lakes oceans sea rain spit

all come to equal some kind of loss

or river stones rounded
cold through and through which also means loss

the feet you can't forget so small
and then wonder Were his pockets empty

Or filled with a dust grove of directions
not splintered from the body

Forget walking and also legs and also the way
the boy would look at you

look at his body
empty after.

ACKNOWLEDGEMENTS

Poems from *Goodbye Lyric* have appeared in *Pilgrimage, Crab Orchard Review, ninth letter, Sou'wester, The Paris-American,* and the anthologies, *The McSweeney's Book of Poets Picking Poets, From the Fishouse: An Anthology of Poems that Sing, Rhyme, Resound, Syncopate, Alliterate, and Just Plain Sound Great,* and *Angles of Ascent: A Norton Anthology of Contemporary African American Poets.*

I extend the deepest thanks to the many readers who have cheered on the gigans in the ten years between their inception and the publication of this manuscript, especially Ross Gay who read each one as it came to be. Thank you as well to Adrian Matejka, and Wendy S. Walters who had regular conversations with me about the form over a period of years. Thank you to those who have taken up the form and published gigans of their own. I am especially grateful to Allison Joseph and Jon Tribble who gave the gigans their first audience in *Crab Orchard Review,* Spring 2006. As always, I am fortunate to have a large and supportive writing family in Cave Canem with too many inspirations to list here. I extend thanks to the University of Missouri-St. Louis, to the Yaddo Foundation, and to the Yaddo fellows of July, 2006 without whom many of these poems would not have come to light. I am grateful for my undergraduate poetry writing students, their ever present questions, and our "poetry of war and resistance" project which led to much of the writing of *Lovely Gun.*

I dedicate this book to Paul Smith, my love, who makes it all seem plausible.